A Year of Terror on the Streets of Phoenix

True Crime Cases of the Serial Killer Shooters and the Baseline Killer

Jack Smith

Copyrights

All rights reserved. © Jack Smith (2017) and Maplewood Publishing (2017). No part of this publication or the information in it may be quoted from or reproduced in any form by means such as printing, scanning, photocopying, or otherwise without prior written permission of the copyright holder.

Disclaimer and Terms of Use

Effort has been made to ensure that the information in this book is accurate and complete. However, the author and the publisher do not warrant the accuracy of the information, text, and graphics contained within the book due to the rapidly changing nature of science, research, known and unknown facts, and internet. The author and the publisher do not hold any responsibility for errors, omissions, or contrary interpretation of the subject matter herein. This book is presented solely for motivational and informational purposes only.

Warning

Throughout the book there are some descriptions of murders and crime scenes that some people might find disturbing. There are also language used by people involved in the murders that may not be appropriate.

ISBN: 978-1986739245

Printed in the United States

MAPLEWOOD
-- PUBLISHING --

Contents

Phoenix, Summer of 2005 — 1
Part I: The Baseline Murderer — 9
  A History of Violence — 9
  A Serial Killer — 13
  The Investigation — 19
  The Trial — 23
  Psychological Analysis — 27
Part II: The Serial Street Shooters — 37
  Shots Fired — 37
  The Killers — 41
  The Investigation — 45
  The Trial — 63
  Psychological Imbalance — 67
Part III: The Aftermath — 75
  Phoenix Reeling — 75
Timeline of Events — 83
Further Readings — 89
Also by Jack Smith — 91

Phoenix, Summer of 2005

In the hot sands of the Arizona desert, the capital city of Phoenix sprawls across the flat lands in between the Rocky Mountains. The area is called the Valley of the Sun, and the tall buildings of Phoenix jut from the center before the city levels out into a wide expanse of one and two story shops and residential areas. Although it's probably better known for its more recreational aspects, Phoenix has a much darker side that has stained the front pages of newspapers with the activity of multiple serial killers for the past decade.

At the end of the summer of 2005, Phoenix was dealing with the unprecedented issue of having two or more serial killers active simultaneously. Although they could distinguish one of them from the others, police would still be unable to make any breakthroughs for over a year. What they did know was that there was a killer who assaulted, raped, robbed, and killed his victims on and around Baseline Road. He was quickly dubbed the Baseline Killer.

The second killer, or killers, was more difficult for police to figure out. He (or they) perpetrated random shootings, some fatal and some not, committed with different weapons. With the crime issues around the city, it was often hard to figure out which shootings were the work of the serial killer(s) and which resulted from gang and drug violence. Even more confusing was the back and forth on whether the Serial Street Shooter was one or more people.

In the year from that summer of 2005 to the summer of 2006, Phoenix would be a bloody mess of murders, assaults, rapes, robberies, and arsons.

An estimated twenty people were injured and eight killed by the Serial Street Shooters, although the number could be much higher, and they had committed other crimes prior to their "year of terror." The Serial Street Shooters also shot horses and dogs, killing at least ten of them, and set two Wal-Marts on fire.

The Baseline Killer already had his own rap sheet and was even on parole when he began his spree. He was responsible for an estimated nine people murdered, around ten raped, and several dozen robbed (including those he raped and/or killed afterward).

All told, at least four dozen people found themselves at the other end of a gun held by one of the three serial killers active in Phoenix—and half did not survive.

The Serial Street Shooters were discovered to be two friends, Dale Hausner and Samuel Dieteman. Both were fascinated with serial killers and murder. The eerie transcripts of them discussing the crimes was chilling evidence of the duo's depravity. Dale's brother Jeff was also believed to have been involved in some of their early shootings, and possibly two other crimes not committed during the Serial Street Shooters rampage.

Mark Goudeau still maintains that he is not the Baseline Killer, despite DNA evidence, evidence found in his home, and even surveillance footage indicating his guilt. His defense claimed that police targeted him because of his race—but conveniently disregarded the mountain of evidence investigators assembled against him.

Ten years later, another serial killer was randomly shooting people in Phoenix, and a city still dealing with the traumatic memory of the Serial Street Shooters once again found itself living in fear. The fear increased when a second shooter—and then several other copycat shooters—popped up as well.

Although the initial copycat was later discovered to be a group of teenagers using BB and pellet rifles to shoot at cars, the fear was rampant, and the media couldn't help but bring up the horror that had occurred from June 2005 to August 2006.

Like most cities, Phoenix, Arizona, has its rough edges. Poverty, gangs, drugs, and petty crime are all issues there. Although Tucson is closer to the Mexican border, Phoenix is close enough to have similar issues with immigrants, both legal and illegal. The influx of people causes a higher demand for jobs and residential space. The number of people who work under the table for very little is high, and the need for low-cost housing is even higher. This means that there are many impoverished families who struggle to get jobs, get housing, and get by.

Crime, of course, is usually more prevalent at the lower end of the economic scale. Meanwhile, depression, stress, and anxiety in such households can lead to substance abuse. Certain substances are addictive enough that their users often resort to crime to get their fix. Theft occurs, whether of cash, pawnable items, or simply the drugs themselves. Large numbers of people involved in crime lead to gangs, which leads to further crime. Phoenix is not immune to this cycle and these issues.

The crimes started as assaults, armed robberies, and arsons. And then there was a woman raped. And then there was a murder. The murders started adding up, as did the other crimes. There were similarities in the locations, witness descriptions, and evidence. But was it one criminal? Two? Three? What was happening in Phoenix?

Animals were shot and killed in backyards, or even while being walked down the street on a leash. Women were found raped and murdered. Random people were shot, some fatally, just walking down the sidewalk. There was no rhyme or reason, no definitive pattern.

Phoenix was terrified. People became afraid to take the bus or walk to a nearby store. Fast food restaurants were haunted by the bodies found in the alleys behind their buildings. Fear took hold as streetwise Phoenicians no longer felt safe outside of their homes.

The police had their hands full, but as the citizens demanded answers, investigators did what they could. There were witnesses stating that some of the shootings were being committed by someone in a light tan or beige colored car. And police determined that they had been using a .22 rifle during the first half of their crime spree. But there was no description of what those shooters looked like.

And then a light-complexioned man of African descent began committing robberies, rapes, and murders. Most often he wore a fishing hat and a wig of dreadlocks, although sometimes he wore other costumes. Was he the one in the car? He didn't use the same weapon, though, so most believed that there were two different criminals.

And then the shooters disappeared for a few months. When the shootings started up again, the weapon was a .410 shotgun. Was this a third killer, or had the first one simply gotten a new gun?

Eventually, authorities decided that an incentive might help with the investigation. Billboards went up offering $100,000 for information leading to the arrest and prosecution of anyone involved in the crimes. That reward—along with guilt—brought in the first big lead on the Serial Street Shooters.

Meanwhile, a man confessed to one of the murders that were now being called the Baseline Killings. However, when police began questioning him about the other crimes, the suspect realized his lack of judgment and recanted his confession—which the police had already decided was false.

With the help of a man who knew one of the killers, they began to close in on the Serial Street Shooters. It wasn't one man, it was two, and sometimes a third. The police wiretapped the apartment of the main suspect, resulting in one of the more chilling conversations ever captured by investigators. The transcript (which can be read in Chapter 8) reveals two men who imbibed alcohol, used meth, and then shot people for fun. They had no real reason or motive, other than to shoot to kill.

Dale Hausner and Samuel Dieteman were the Serial Street Shooters, although it is theorized that originally it was Dale and his brother, Jeff Hausner, and then Dieteman came in as the shooter at the third murder. Jeff Hausner then became less involved due to work and other issues, and Dieteman and Dale Hausner continued their rampage. On several nights, the shootings of animals and people, robberies of fast food restaurants, and even arsons went on for hours.

When they were first questioned, Dieteman spilled everything to the police while Hausner held out. Eventually, however, Hausner not only admitted to his crimes, he asked for the death penalty. Apparently he couldn't wait for the State of Arizona to carry it out, though, as he took his own life in prison several years after his sentencing.

Meanwhile, a very astute member of the Arizona parole board saw the sketches of the Baseline Killer and recognized his modus operandi of robbery, rape, and assault. The board sent the task force their information on Mark Goudeau. Goudeau had served half of his prison term for the brutal assault and rape of a woman, and the Baseline Killer had become active after his release on parole.

Luckily for investigators, Goudeau's DNA was on file due to his previous crimes. It matched one of the double assault-and-rapes attributed to the Baseline Killer. With that information and a bit more digging, authorities obtained a warrant and were quickly able to identify Goudeau as their killer.

Although he and his wife both swore that he was innocent, there was no denying the evidence. The fact of his previous arrest, as well as dropped charges in other rapes and assaults, obviously didn't help Goudeau's case. His wife's credibility took a nosedive when she vehemently said he was not a cocaine user—even though he had admitted to the habit on several occasions (including at his first trial for robbery years before) and was found to have the substance on him at the time of his arrest.

Ten years later, Phoenix would relive the previous nightmare as someone began shooting at cars on the major interstate and highways in the city. As it became clear that there was another serial shooter, several young people began committing copycat crimes using non-lethal weapons such as pellet guns and sling shots. Once again, Phoenix was in fear. No one was killed in the new string of shootings, but that relief was short lived. Another serial killer, Aaron Saucedo, soon popped up, and he shot and killed nine people, including women and children.

The I-10 Shooter operated from mid-August to mid-September in 2015, while Saucedo's attacks spanned from August 2015 to July 2016. As with the Serial Street Shooters, Saucedo's victims were random people out on the streets, walking down the sidewalks and minding their own business. Some were even inside their homes when the shooter drove by and unleashed his bullets. In addition to the nine murders, Saucedo committed at least three other attacks; however, investigators are still compiling information on the case, as they believe there could be more crimes tied to him.

The recent resurgence of serial shooters in Phoenix has brought up memories of the "year of fear" in 2005 to 2006. News channels, blogs, social media, and various crime reporters have once again been bringing up the Serial Street Shooters and the Baseline Killer. Discussions about the prevalence of crime in the city and questions about the active serial killers roaming about have been daily conversation since the shootings that started up in 2015.

Reading this, it may seem like Phoenix is some kind of serial killer capital, but of course it's far from the only city to be plagued by this brand of crime. As news is able to travel faster and reach further, what used to be local news is now internationally known. The realization that serial killers are more common than we ever knew is alarming, but it isn't actually a new issue. In 2005, though, social media was just getting off the ground. The stories of the Baseline Killer and the Serial Street Shooters spread much more slowly than those of the 2015 serial shooters. But now it is easier than ever to go back and see the comparisons with what happened in Phoenix, Arizona, in the summer of 2005.

Part I: The Baseline Murderer

A History of Violence

Born on September 6, 1964, to Willie and Alberta Goudeau, Mark Goudeau was the second-to-last child of thirteen the couple would have. The last sibling would be a younger brother. He grew up in Phoenix with his six brothers and six sisters. Though there is some argument amongst his siblings as to the truth of their childhood, many of them agree that there were issues with drugs, alcohol, and a tough and domineering father. Before her death when Mark was thirteen, Alberta worked as a maid. His father was a lot attendant at area car lots.

In high school, Mark Goudeau was a football player, as was his younger brother. The brother, though, went on to play for a local college whereas Mark never completed high school. His first run-in with the law occurred when he was eighteen, and he would continue to have legal trouble for the rest of his life. He wasn't alone in that; out of the thirteen Goudeau children, at least six would become felons. Four have served serious prison time at penitentiaries, two are currently in prison, and another went on parole around the time of Goudeau's final incarceration. Goudeau himself was out on good behavior prior to the Baseline killings.

In 1982, Goudeau and one of his brothers were arrested for the assault and rape of a woman. Shortly afterward, the woman dropped the charges. At the time, it was assumed that fear was the reason she decided to recant her previous claims. Mark Goudeau was in trouble with the law again in 1987 on a trespassing charge stemming from a heated and violent argument at a bar. In 1988, he was charged with an alcohol violation. And then his crimes became much more serious.

In August of 1989, a woman named Darlene Fernandez came forward claiming that Goudeau had beaten and raped her multiple times over two days. After raping her, he tried to force cocaine up her nose. Then, in a fit of anger, he beat her with a barbell, followed by a shotgun. Next he threw her in the bathtub, possibly to wash away the evidence of the rape. Afterward, in a parking lot, he beat her again and chased two witnesses away from the scene.

For his part, Goudeau claimed he and Fernandez had gone into a hotel for consensual oral sex and decided to take a bath together. While they were in the bathtub, two men forced open the door and held him at gunpoint while they beat the woman. Although his story contradicted hers, he did plead no contest to aggravated assault.

While awaiting sentencing in August of 1990, Goudeau went to a Fry's supermarket at the intersection of 30th Street and Thomas Road. Inside, he held the female cashier at gunpoint and demanded all of the money she could get him. The total would be $850. He then made all of the employees line up and walked them outside at gunpoint before being stopped. His excuse was that he needed money for his crack cocaine habit.

At his sentencing, Mark Goudeau was given 15 years for assault and 21 years for armed robbery, to run consecutively for a total of 21 years. But in 2004, after serving only 13 years of his sentence, Goudeau was released on good behavior.

He told the parole board that he had learned his lesson and was hoping to turn over a new leaf by pursuing an honest career in construction. Goudeau's wife, Wendy Carr, also spoke on his behalf. She assured the parole board that he was a new man and would never be back in the same position ever again. She pleaded with them to give him a chance to show how much he had improved and how he could be a useful asset to society. As Goudeau had been a model inmate while incarcerated, the parole board believed their statements and granted him his freedom. Little did they know the mistake they were making.

While Goudeau had been in prison, Wendy had purchased a modest home in a decent neighborhood. After his release, he moved in with her and soon began working for a construction company. He began to settle into an outward routine of working, building a family, and doing exactly as he'd told the parole board he would do. His neighbors said he seemed like a family man, a loving husband, and an all-around good guy.

But Mark Goudeau had a Hyde to go with his Jekyll. He was a cocaine user and abuser who often sought the company of other women—prostitutes, fellow drug users, and even friends of his family. As much as his wife protested that he was a "family man" and couldn't possibly be the Baseline Killer, Mark Goudeau's activities outside of his home, and away from his wife and children, said much differently. And when he was caught, the evidence spoke volumes as to who Mark Goudeau really was.

A Serial Killer

To all appearances, Mark Goudeau was doing well. And then the assaults began.

Baseline Road was the starting point of one of the serial killers active in Phoenix in the latter half of 2005. His first crimes were not murders, but the escalation began soon enough. Serial killers often start small and build up; the same is true of drug abusers. Mark Goudeau was both. His sexual assaults on women had begun in his teenage years and escalated later to his brutal beating and rape of Darlene Fernandez. Once Goudeau was free, he picked up where he'd left off and continued to become increasingly violent. Eventually, beating and raping the women was not enough. Mark Goudeau began to kill.

A church near Baseline Road, on 48th Street, became the scene of the Baseline Killer's first crime on August 6, 2005. Three teenage girls were outside the church when they were approached by a man with a gun. He ordered them around to the back of the building and held them at gunpoint while he molested two of them. As the girls were underage, their information was not released to the public, but their attacker was described as a "light-colored man of color."

The next incident was a robbery on Thomas Road. On August 14, at around four in the morning, a woman was held at gunpoint and raped before being robbed by a man with a description similar to that given by the three teenagers. Almost a month later, on September 9, the body of 19-year-old Georgia Thompson was discovered on Mill Avenue. She had died from a gunshot wound. On September 15, a woman was sexually assaulted at gunpoint on 40th Street.

The varying nature of these crimes was what originally made it so difficult for investigators to figure out that the incidents were connected. As it happened, the next crime, committed on September 20, was the one that would eventually allow police to determine that Mark Goudeau was their culprit.

That day, two sisters were walking home on Vineyard Road when they were approached by a man with a gun. One of the women was visibly pregnant, and the man, later identified as Goudeau, kept his gun pressed into her stomach as he sexually assaulted and raped them both.

At one point, Goudeau had difficulties maintaining his erection while attempting to put on a condom. One of the women was able to grab his gun and turn it on him. However, whether because the safety was on or because she had never held a firearm before, she was unable to pull the trigger, and Goudeau got the gun back. He then pressed it against her genitalia while threatening their lives.

Before fleeing, he forced the women to spit in his hand and then he scooped up mud and mixed it with the saliva before rubbing the mixture on parts of their bodies he had been in contact with. This was apparently an attempt to destroy DNA evidence. However, the women's witness statements and Goudeau's DNA were both collected. Unfortunately, they would not be processed for over nine months due to an evidentiary backlog. This lapse would allow Goudeau's rampage to continue and to escalate, and also result in a lawsuit from the families of the Baseline Killer's later victims.

Two robberies were committed on September 28. One was on Baseline Road itself; the other was on Central Avenue, where a woman was sexually assaulted and then robbed. By now, the perpetrator of all these crimes was beginning to match up. He was a light-colored man of African descent, wore a floppy hat like fishermen wore, and had dreadlocks.

On November 3, the same man committed several robberies and sexual assaults throughout the day. The first was a robbery on 32nd Street that morning. Ten minutes later, a woman across the street from that crime scene was sexually assaulted. Shortly after that, a dreadlocked man with a fisherman's hat robbed an adult store, Cupid's Toy Box, on 32nd Street North of $720. Within another ten minutes, a woman was abducted from near a donation bin across from that robbery. She was sexually assaulted and forced to drive her attacker to another location because he had just robbed the store nearby.

Four days later, on November 7, the Baseline Killer went on another robbery spree on 32nd Street. He started at Las Brasas Mexican Restaurant and then moved to Little Caesar's Pizza Place, robbing both the eateries and the patrons. After he was done inside, he went out to the street and proceeded to rob four more people. He even fired his gun in the air as he threatened them.

On December 12, the second murder occurred on 40th Street. 39-year-old Tina Washington, a preschool teacher, was on her way home from work when she was accosted by a man with a gun. A witness, Peter Ochoa, originally assumed that the two gunshots he heard were the sounds of kids throwing something or playing in the alley behind his restaurant. Going out to investigate, he saw the killer crouched over Washington's body, still holding the gun. The man then pointed the weapon at him and pulled the trigger, but it misfired. Ochoa hurried back inside and locked the door. The gunman tried to get in, but eventually gave up. The Baseline Rapist officially became the Baseline Killer, and there was officially a serial killer on the loose in Phoenix.

After another robbery on December 13, the Baseline Killer went quiet for two months. He returned on February 20, 2006, with the double murder of Romelia Vargas, 38, and Mirna Palma-Roman, 34, inside a food truck. However, the killings were assumed to be drug-related and were not linked to the Baseline Killer for several more months.

After Goudeau's conviction, the family of Romelia Vargas sued the Phoenix Police Department for her death on the grounds that earlier processing of the DNA evidence in the rape of the two sisters would have prevented all deaths that came afterward, including that of Romelia Vargas. They did not win their case.

Another double homicide on March 15 was attributed to the Baseline Killer. Liliana Sanchez-Cabrera and Chao Chou were kidnapped at gunpoint on their way home from work at Yoshi's Restaurant on 24th Street. The body of 20-year-old Liliana Sanchez-Cabrera was found in the parking lot of a fast food restaurant; Chao Chou was found over a mile away. Both victims had died from gunshot wounds to the head.

On March 29, police were called to a parking lot on 24th Street when a man found blood in the gravel. Although they did a preliminary search, nothing more was found. The lot baked under the hot Arizona sun for another week before a foul odor pushed the original informant to search it more thoroughly. When he did, he discovered the body of Kristin Nicole Gibbons.

Sophia Nunez was found deceased in her bathtub from a gunshot wound by her 7-year-old son on April 10. She had taken the day off to participate in an immigration reform march. When her son was released from school, though, she was not there to pick him up. The boy then walked all the way home. The garage door wasn't all the way down and so he was able to wiggle underneath. Upon searching the house for his mother, he noticed water coming out from under the door to the bathroom. Sophia Nunez was in an overflowing tub, partially nude, with two bullet holes in her head. It is an image her child will never unsee. Investigators initially suspected her ex-husband, but his alibi checked out. When Goudeau was arrested, his cell phone records connected him to Nunez.

On May 1, outside the same restaurants he had robbed months before, the Baseline Killer kidnapped a woman at gunpoint and sexually assaulted her in her car. She would later testify:

He asked me to touch myself. At that point, I realized it was going to be a rape, and I was afraid to die… He said, "Suck my dick," and he was going to kill me if I didn't. I said, "Go ahead and kill me." He said he was going to blow my brains out in the car and my parents were going to read about it in the newspaper the next day. He pulled the trigger and there was a loud clinking noise. I realized that I wasn't dead, and so I got out of my vehicle and ran.

The Baseline Killer's last crime, a homicide, was captured on surveillance cameras. On June 29, 37-year-old Carmen Miranda was on her cell phone at a carwash on Thomas Road when she was approached by a man with a gun. The video is too grainy for a definitive identification, but it shows the man approaching her, pointing a gun at her, and walking her off camera. Her body was later found approximately 100 yards away behind a barbershop with a gunshot wound to the head.

The Investigation

The investigation into the Baseline Killer case had several issues to deal with.

One of the first problems came with the false confession of a man police had in custody. James Dewayne Mullins confessed on September 2, 2005, that he had shot and killed Georgia Thompson. He told detectives that he had shot her outside of a strip club where she was working. This was the first clue that Mullins was lying: Thompson was found where she was shot, which was outside the front door of her apartment, several blocks from where she worked. It wasn't until her case was connected to the Baseline Killer's other murders that Mullins recanted and admitted he had not killed her.

With the Serial Street Shooters active at the same time, there was a plethora of ongoing investigations in Phoenix. On top of the simultaneously operating serial killers, there were also the everyday drug and gang related crimes. And while the Serial Street Shooters' crimes were linked by the vehicle they used, the Baseline Killer was either on foot or riding a bicycle. This, combined with the fact that his crimes varied between robbery, assault, rape, and murder, meant that his crimes initially seemed like separate incidents of drug or gang violence.

When the police sketches and witness statements made it to the state parole board, however, they contacted the Phoenix Police Department. They knew of a man who not only looked like the sketches but had a history that matched up with some of the crimes committed by the Baseline Killer. They suggested that police look into Mark Goudeau. The police went to Goudeau's home, and upon finding a mask described in earlier witness statements and a toy gun, they were able to get a search warrant for the house.

As the police began collecting evidence at the Goudeau residence, items containing specks of the victims' blood and guns which matched the ballistic evidence tightened their case even more. Arizona had found the Baseline Killer.

During Goudeau's rape of the two sisters, he had made them spit in his hand and then mixed their saliva with mud before smearing it on them in an attempt to eliminate any DNA evidence. At one point, his idea might have worked. But DNA analysis had advanced a bit further than Mark Goudeau knew. Technicians were able to isolate the DNA in the mixture that had a Y chromosome (only found in males). They could thus differentiate between the mixed samples and extract the one from the male rapist for sequencing. Due to a backlog of cases, it took a year, but they were finally able to confirm that the male DNA belonged to Mark Goudeau.

There is a real possibility that several of his victims would still be alive if the case had been processed faster.

Goudeau was arrested on September 6, 2006, on his forty-second birthday, as he exited his vehicle when he arrived home from work. He was taken in without incident by the same cop who had arrested him over a decade before for the crimes that sent him to prison. He wasn't carrying any weapons, although he did have crack cocaine and a cell phone in his pockets. However, the DNA evidence was enough for police to lock Goudeau up so they could proceed to investigate him as the Baseline Killer.

The first additional evidence that surfaced connected Goudeau to a case that police had not yet lumped in with the Baseline murders, that of Sophia Nunez. According to cell phone records, Goudeau had called Sophia Nunez on a multitude of occasions, to the point of obsessive calling.

Alicia Bell, Nunez's aunt, told police that Nunez had met Goudeau in a bar. He had pretended to be a disabled baseball player, but Nunez had not fallen for the lie. She told her family that she knew he was married and that he seemed very weird to her; he made her uncomfortable. Goudeau kept contacting Nunez, attempting to hook up. Nunez, though, was not interested, and eventually Goudeau left her alone.

Unfortunately, that did not mean he was finished pursuing her. DNA evidence found on her breast matched Goudeau's DNA. The bullet removed from her head was of the same caliber and had striations matching those from the other murders, linking her to the Baseline Killer—and thus linking Goudeau to the case.

Goudeau's shoes also assisted in the case. The white Nikes had blood droplets from both Kristin Nicole Gibbons and Chao Chou. Gibbons's DNA was also found in five blood droplets from high-velocity back-spatter on a black ski mask recovered from Goudeau's home. Also found was the ring Tina Washington had on prior to her murder, with her three sons names engraved on it. Other jewelry matching other victims was found in a Ziploc bag in one of Goudeau's shoes.

Goudeau was now facing over eighty charges ranging from possession of a scheduled substance (because of the cocaine found on him at the time of his arrest) to robbery, assault, kidnapping, rape, and nine murders.

Nevertheless, and despite the DNA evidence, witness statements, and Goudeau's history of robbery, assault, attempted murder, and rape, not everyone saw him as a viable suspect. His wife, Wendy Carr, was adamant that the police were either railroading him in an effort to close the case or simply targeting him due to his race.

The Trial

Trial of the first case, that of the two sisters who were kidnapped, assaulted and raped on September 20, 2005, began on July 23, 2007. The confirmation that Goudeau's DNA had been recovered from the victims would seem to be enough to prove the 19 charges leveled against him, but there were some issues.

Because of how Goudeau had the women smear their own saliva and mud over his DNA, it took an experimental procedure to isolate the Y chromosome DNA from the mixture. The procedure used up the entire sample, leaving none for the defense to examine with their own specialists. The defense also pointed out that the DNA could technically be from one of Goudeau's immediate male family members—many of whom had criminal records of their own.

There was also an incident in which one of the witnesses accidentally identified Goudeau's attorney as her attacker instead of Goudeau himself.

In the end, though, the story the sisters told, including Goudeau pressing his weapon to the pregnant sister's genitals and threatening her life and the life of the child within her, had the expected effect on the jury. They felt confident enough to find Goudeau guilty even without knowing about his connection to the Baseline Murders; they had purposefully been kept in the dark to prevent the possibility of a mistrial or other issues on appeal.

Goudeau was sentenced to 438 years upon being convicted of kidnapping, assault, aggravated assault, rape, weapons violations, and possession.

Goudeau's second trial, covering 74 different charges that included nine cases of first-degree murder, didn't begin until July of 2011. The trial spanned a full four months and was separated into thirteen segments, each focusing on a scene or major crime. Witnesses included rape victims, robbery victims, and the friends and families of victims. Detailed and emotional descriptions of Mark Goudeau's words, his actions, the way he had pressed his gun to his victims, and the threats and feelings during the crimes weighed heavily not just on the jury but on the investigators and other victims.

Those who found the bodies described what they saw and what they felt. Peter Ochoa went back over his account of discovering Mark Goudeau hovering over the body of Tina Washington. He had been less than ten feet from the killer when Goudeau tried to shoot him, but the gun misfired. "I will never forget those eyes, never," Peter Ochoa told the jury as he pointed out Mark Goudeau as the man he had seen that night.

Protesting his innocence, Goudeau claimed the investigators were biased, using his past to decide who he was. He claimed he had been clean ever since he was released from prison. However, there were red flags in his declarations: He referred to himself in the third person, repeated the same sentences over and over, and blamed his attorneys (as well as everyone else) for failing him and being against him.

Mark Goudeau was found guilty of 67 felonies on October 31, 2011—Halloween. These included all nine murders attributed to the Baseline Killer. On November 30, he was sentenced to death.

Goudeau appealed his conviction, arguing that each of the nine murders should have been tried independently. The appeals court found no reason for this and upheld the original ruling and sentencing for the murders and other felonies. To this day, Mark Goudeau and his wife, Wendy Carr, still claim he is innocent and are continuing the appeals process.

Part of their reasoning involves James Dewayne Mullins's confession to the murder of Georgia Thompson. But the murders of Romelia Vargas and Mirna Palma-Roman in February of 2006 also had a different suspect originally. That man, Terry Wayne Smith, looks very similar to Mark Goudeau, and thus the sketch of the Baseline Killer could easily depict Smith instead of Goudeau. A lengthy document from one of the officers investigating the Baseline case describes how Smith, like Goudeau, was released from prison shortly before the murders began. He also had a multitude of past charges, including rape and assault, and was suspected in at least two other homicides. When he was arrested several days after Goudeau, he held his family at gunpoint (for which he received a prison sentence).

Their personal similarities are striking, and there is some unbiased speculation that the two could have collaborated on at least some crimes. However, there is no evidence tying them together, and Smith has been officially dismissed as a suspect in any of the Baseline murders.

Psychological Analysis

The Baseline Killer's function was one of fast, primal rage. He raped, he assaulted, and sometimes he killed.

In the absence of psychiatric evaluations and mental health records from his youth, much can be discerned from his crimes, lifestyle, and, most definitively, his behavior and words in court.

Several factors contributed to the transformation of small-time criminal Mark Goudeau into the Baseline Killer. Negative influences on Goudeau's behavior date back to his childhood. On top of that, he had issues with his mental health that were reflected in his abuse of drugs and his feelings toward the people around him.

Goudeau's father was described as a disciplinarian, a stern man, an alcoholic, and there were rumors of drug abuse. His mother passed away shortly before he reached his teenage years. On top of this, Goudeau was one of thirteen children, the second youngest, in a low-income household. His mother was a maid and his father was a lot attendant, so they weren't receiving large paychecks. More than half of Goudeau's siblings had multiple run-ins with the law, some as early as their teen years. His own first major crime (one of those for which the charges were dropped) was committed with his brother. Stealing and violence were commonplace to Mark Goudeau from an early age.

And then there were the drugs. Mark Goudeau was a cocaine user. His thefts, by his own admission, were usually in pursuit of drug money. Cocaine has notable effects on the human brain, and thus has an obvious effect on the behavior of the user. Outside of the addiction and the need to constantly obtain more cocaine to stay high, there are mood swings and a tendency towards anger and violence. Both the drug and the withdrawal from the drug cause similar, often violent behavior.

At the time of his arrest, Mark Goudeau had crack cocaine on his person. He had a history of cocaine use. Before his first trial for assault and rape back in the 90s, he had robbed a store in order to purchase more cocaine. He was already looking at jail time, and yet instead of lying low he committed another crime just to score again.

Cocaine is highly addictive. One of the issues with the drug is how it damages the reward system in the brain. At first, the dopamine dumps caused by the drug give a nearly euphoric feeling. That, along with the racing heartbeat and higher blood pressure, is what makes the initial highs feel so seductive. And yet, the more someone takes it, both in quantity and frequency, the more they will need to take to get a similar feeling. This becomes the loop of addiction.

Because of the deficit of "feel-good" chemicals in the brain, irritability and anger issues begin to emerge. For someone already used to and prone to violence, cocaine can enhance these feelings and create an amplification in violent outbursts.

When a patient is using cocaine excessively, there is little difficulty in arriving at the diagnosis of cocaine dependence. According to the American Psychiatric Association's Diagnostic and Statistical Manual of Mental Disorders, Fourth Edition (DSM-IV), only three of the following conditions must be present:

- *Developing tolerance to the euphoric effects of cocaine and requiring more drug to produce the desired effects.*
- *Stopping cocaine usually results in withdrawal symptoms (such as fatigue, sleep disturbances, agitation, or depression), and these symptoms can be relieved by using cocaine again.*
- *Using cocaine in large amounts whenever it is available. (Seldom do people save some for later.)*

- *Inability to successfully reduce the amount of cocaine one is using.*
- *Spending a great deal of time and energy obtaining and using cocaine, which isolates one from friends and family, and/or engaging in unlawful activities such as shoplifting, theft, burglary, or homicide to obtain money to buy cocaine.*
- *Inability to successfully maintain employment while using cocaine because of ineffectiveness at work, increased absenteeism, inability to hold a job, or inability to find work.*
- *Continually using cocaine despite knowing one will develop mental symptoms, such as paranoia, hallucinations, and delusions, and/or continually using cocaine despite medical consequences, such as weight loss, anemia, or seizures.*

Additional psychiatric disorders can accompany the diagnosis of cocaine dependence. These can include cocaine intoxication, cocaine withdrawal, cocaine intoxication delirium, cocaine-induced psychotic disorders with hallucination and/or delusions, cocaine-induced mood disorder, cocaine-induced anxiety disorder, cocaine-induced sexual dysfunction, and cocaine-induced sleep disorder.

Cocaine use has also been associated with homicide. In New York City, 31% of 2,824 homicide victims tested positive for cocaine or its metabolite, benzoylecgonine. A significant number (27%) of NYC residents who succumbed to fatal injuries also tested positive for cocaine. Fatal injuries secondary to homicide accounted for 29% of these victims. Concurrent drug use, including alcohol and marijuana, was cited as an additional factor in this report. Other cities have reported similar disturbing findings. One study found that 18% of homicide victims in New Orleans tested positive for cocaine. In Los Angeles, 61% of autopsied individuals who tested positive for cocaine had died violently. (www.ncbi.nlm.nih.gov)

As addicts struggle to obtain more cocaine, or deal with other situations like mental illness, their anger becomes more commonplace. In Mark Goudeau's case, though, his wife and neighbors never mentioned that he was prone to anger, much less violence. There are several possible reasons for this.

The first may stem from household dynamics. Both in low-income households and in those with active drug users, there tend to be unspoken rules and expectations about violence. This is not universal, as many low-income families function without any issues of violence, but once drugs and alcohol are involved, the situation changes. Those involved tend to stay quiet rather than reporting each other. For some it is fear, for others pride, and then there are those who do not see domestic violence as abnormal or significant.

Another consideration is that of battered woman syndrome (BWS). *BWS is a mental disorder that develops in victims of domestic violence as a result of serious, long-term abuse. BWS is dangerous primarily because it can lead to "learned helplessness"—or psychological paralysis—where the victim becomes so depressed, defeated, and passive that she believes she is incapable of leaving the abusive situation. Though this may seem irrational, it feels absolutely real to the victim. Feeling fearful and weak, and sometimes even still holding onto the hope that her abuser will stop hurting her, the victim remains in the home, continuing the cycle of domestic violence and strengthening her existing BWS.*
(http://family.findlaw.com/domestic-violence/battered-women-s-syndrome.html)

One unproven theory states that in these situations, the spouse and the children may be so accustomed to the violence and feel such empathy towards the abuser that they feel that doing something about the situation would be a betrayal. They stay silent because they see themselves as a family unit. They formulate excuses, make exceptions, and construct a wall of lies that are believed by both the abuser and the victims.

The other reason that most people saw Mark Goudeau as a nonviolent man, a good man, was that he put on that mask. Goudeau had a type of antisocial personality disorder, although not the actual Antisocial Personality Disorder or APD. To the layman, he is what is called a psychopath.

Psychopathy is a disorder characterized by pronounced emotional deficits, marked by reduction in guilt and empathy, and involves increased risk for displaying antisocial behavior. The disorder is developmental. Psychopathic traits, particularly the emotional component, are relatively stable from childhood into adulthood. One reason for the attention this classification receives is its strong predictive utility for institutional adjustment and recidivism (i.e., reoffending). Individuals with psychopathy are approximately three times more likely to reoffend than those with low psychopathic traits, and four times more likely to reoffend violently. Admittedly, it is the past antisocial behavior, indexed by psychopathy assessments, that is particularly important in predicting future criminal activity. However, it is the emotional component that characterizes psychopathy; high levels of antisocial behavior can develop from other neurobiological and socio-environmental risk factors. Psychopathy is not equivalent to the DSM-IV diagnosis of conduct disorder or antisocial personality disorder (ASPD) or their ICD-10 counterparts. The psychiatric diagnoses focus on antisocial behavior rather than underlying causes; i.e., the emotion dysfunction seen in psychopathy. As a consequence, individuals meeting the criteria for antisocial personality disorder are more heterogeneous in their pathophysiology than individuals meeting criteria for psychopathy.
(www.ncbi.nlm.nih.gov)

There is a dissonance between Mark Goudeau and other people. He doesn't register emotions the same way other people do. Despite this disconnection, Goudeau still has strong emotions himself. This is the difference between a sociopath and a psychopath. His moods can swing wildly from depression to anger, and anything in between. He also has an uncanny ability to lie convincingly because he doesn't feel guilt as someone with a stable mentality would.

This means that he could put on an act for his neighbors and those around them and it would seem genuine. It could also mean that if there was no violence in his home, it was because he had the ability to repress that personality when with his wife and children, thereby showing a more extensive level of psychopathy.

Habitual lying, to the point of nearly convincing himself that he is telling the truth, as well as self-preservation built upon ingrained narcissism, are further components of his persona. This was clearly displayed after his trial when he stated: "They assassinated my character. They painted me as a monster. I am no monster. Mark Goudeau is no monster. I am no monster."

His reference to himself in the third person is a distinguishing mark of someone who has an inward disconnection. Although this quirk is sometimes seen in people with mental issues that cause lower intelligence, it is also extremely common in those who display arrogance and narcissism. Introducing a separation between himself and his name is also a tactic to make the habitual lying easier. By creating a character known as Mark Goudeau, he is able to keep the fiction up; being himself merely means he is in character for the story he has created.

Goudeau had some siblings with criminal records and some without. Out of all of them, what made him become a serial rapist and then a killer?

The rapes were most likely an extreme reaction to a life with an overbearing male figure, the absence of a mother figure, and a narcissistic belief that he could take what he wanted capped with the psychopathic trait of not feeling remorse for the victims. He saw women as weaker than him, easy to overcome. He saw what he took from them as something he had the right to take. His skewed sense of self was his guide, and they were nothing to him.

Murder, the next step, was merely a mixture of a need for power, mental instability, and self-preservation. The Mayo Clinic explains narcissistic personalities as follows:

Narcissistic personality disorder—one of several types of personality disorders—is a mental condition in which people have an inflated sense of their own importance, a deep need for excessive attention and admiration, troubled relationships, and a lack of empathy for others. But behind this mask of extreme confidence lies a fragile self-esteem that's vulnerable to the slightest criticism.

A narcissistic personality disorder causes problems in many areas of life, such as relationships, work, school or financial affairs. People with narcissistic personality disorder may be generally unhappy and disappointed when they're not given the special favors or admiration they believe they deserve. They may find their relationships unfulfilling, and others may not enjoy being around them.

Signs and symptoms of narcissistic personality disorder and the severity of symptoms vary. People with the disorder can:

- *Have an exaggerated sense of self-importance*
- *Have a sense of entitlement and require constant, excessive admiration*
- *Expect to be recognized as superior even without achievements that warrant it*
- *Exaggerate achievements and talents*
- *Be preoccupied with fantasies about success, power, brilliance, beauty or the perfect mate*
- *Believe they are superior and can only associate with equally special people*
- *Monopolize conversations and belittle or look down on people they perceive as inferior*
- *Expect special favors and unquestioning compliance with their expectations*
- *Take advantage of others to get what they want*
- *Have an inability or unwillingness to recognize the needs and feelings of others*
- *Be envious of others and believe others envy them*
- *Behave in an arrogant or haughty manner, coming across as conceited, boastful and pretentious*
- *Insist on having the best of everything—for instance, the best car or office*

At the same time, people with narcissistic personality disorder have trouble handling anything they perceive as criticism, and they can:

- *Become impatient or angry when they don't receive special treatment*
- *Have significant interpersonal problems and easily feel slighted*
- *React with rage or contempt and try to belittle the other person to make themselves appear superior*

- *Have difficulty regulating emotions and behavior*
- *Experience major problems dealing with stress and adapting to change*
- *Feel depressed and moody because they fall short of perfection*
- *Have secret feelings of insecurity, shame, vulnerability and humiliation*

Some serial killers want the world to know what they are doing, how smart they are compared to those who hunt them. Mark Goudeau, on the other hand, wasn't more intelligent than those who hunted him, and he knew that. In his case, narcissism is what provoked his declarations of innocence. It is a way to try and convince the world that he is innocent, despite the overwhelming evidence of his guilt. He has become so at ease with his own lies, and so used to manipulating people, that he believes his constant denials of guilt and accusations of racism will ultimately result in his convictions being overturned.

Unfortunately for Mark Goudeau, the science of forensics is not susceptible to the lies of man.

Part II: The Serial Street Shooters

Shots Fired

Horses and dogs in the Phoenix area began to turn up injured or deceased from gunshot wounds. Fast food restaurants were shot up and robbed. All the while, people were dropping on the sidewalks, shot by a gunman in a light colored car. At first, these incidents were not connected, but they were in fact the work of a serial killer. Only it wasn't one man, or even two—at some moments three men were actively terrorizing one area of Phoenix as a team, while another man did the same on his own solo spree.

The first murder by the Serial Street Shooters occurred in early May of 2005. Several horses were shot during the day. Then, that evening, Tony Mendez borrowed a trailer from his friend Marcos Portillo to take candles, water, and other supplies to his family, who didn't have electricity. He attached the trailer to his bicycle and headed down the sidewalk.

Several hours later, the body of a man was found slumped across a bicycle attached to a trailer on the same sidewalk. Neighbors, recognizing the trailer, at first thought the man was Portillo. When Portillo came out to see what the fuss was, people were surprised to see him! After they recovered from their shock and explained what was going on, Portillo knew who it was right away. Police soon arrived, and 39-year-old Tony Mendez was pronounced dead from a .22 gunshot wound.

A few weeks later, Reginald Remillard, a 56-year-old veteran, was found on a bus bench where he often napped at 7th Avenue and Camelback. He was also dead from a gunshot wound. On June 29, a quarter horse was found shot to death. Shortly after that, a family was leaving a Jack-in-the-Box fast food eatery when they saw a dead man on the sidewalk. 20-year-old David Estrada had been killed with a .22 rifle. As officers converged on the scene, it was discovered that a nearby Burger King had been shot at and robbed. However, the three crimes wouldn't be connected for almost a year.

July of 2005 started with more horses shot with a .22. Some were found dead; some died later from their injuries. The first horse attack, back in May, was assumed to be the work of someone with a grudge or anger issues. The second was harder to explain away as a simple act of revenge or expression of anger, and as the corpses of horses and dogs continued to pile up, Phoenix began to take notice.

Crime was not an uncommon thing, and the city had experienced its share of shootings, robberies, and even animal cruelty before. But in 2005, the level of all three was noticeably higher. There were two distinct weapons being used. The horses were matching up with the bodies found on the sidewalks. The Baseline rapist had been upgraded to the Baseline Killer, and now more people were being shot by someone else. Phoenix was demanding answers, and the police were scratching their heads.

As we know now, the Serial Street Shooters were Dale Hausner and Samuel Dieteman, sometimes accompanied by Dale's brother Jeff. On November 11, according to Dieteman, Nathaniel Schoffner got into an argument with Dale Hausner. Hausner began shouting at Schoffner, and Schoffner threw something at Hausner. Hausner pulled out the .22 rifle and attempted to shoot Schoffner, only to have it misfire. Hausner then grabbed a sawed-off .410 shotgun and shot Schoffner dead.

December 29 was a night of mayhem in Phoenix. The carnage began around 7:30 that evening with shots being fired near a bartending school. Shortly after, a man walking his dog was stunned when someone driving by shot and killed the animal. Then the Serial Street Shooters turned to human targets. 44-year-old Jose Ortiz was shot and killed. 28-year-old Marco Carillo was shot and killed. A woman named Barbara Whitener was shot but survived. Timmy Tordai was shot in the neck but survived. As the night continued, three more dogs were shot. As the calendar clicked over into December 30, Clarissa Rowley, 21, was shot but survived. All of the attacks were committed by a man in a light tan car who shot at people walking down the sidewalk. At the time, police assumed he was acting alone.

After this spree in the final days of 2005, the killers went quiet. Dieteman later told investigators that this was because Jeff Hausner had gotten a job and wasn't available to go on the rides. It is assumed that the .22 rifle was destroyed during this hiatus as well.

During the Serial Street Shooters' downtime, the Baseline Killer was busy creating his own trail of death.

And then the drive-by shootings began again. As they featured a .410 shotgun instead of the .22 rifle used in the previous shootings, authorities initially thought there was a new, third serial killer. They hadn't given a name to the one in the pale colored car, but they referred to the perpetrator of the second string of killings as the Serial Street Shooter until they realized the connection.

On May 2, 2006, a man driving a light colored car leaned across his passenger with a sawed-off shotgun and killed Kibili Tamadul. Within the hour, the car made a sharp U-turn so the passenger could use the gun to shoot Claudia Gutierrez-Cruz.

The 21-year-old woman begged those who found her to call her sister as she lay bleeding in the street. She died in the hospital.

The next several months saw a slew of pedestrians shot with the same sawed-off shotgun, but miraculously they all survived. On May 17, Timothy Davenport was stabbed in the back and his face slashed with a knife; Dieteman was later charged with this assault. On May 30, Hames Hodge was shot. Miguel Rodriguez and Daryl Davies were both shot in the side on May 31. On June 8, two Wal-Marts in Glendale were set on fire by arsonists. No one was killed in the blazes. That evening, Paul Patrick was shot in his right side. June 11 was the day Elizabeth Clark was shot in the left hip. On June 20, Frederic Cena was shot, and Tony Long was shot in the torso. Diane Bein and Jeremy Ortiz were shot on July 11. Joseph Roberts was shot on July 3, David Perez on the seventh. On July 8 Ashley Armenta was shot in the back of the head but nevertheless survived. Garry Begay was also shot. On July 11, Michael Cordrey was shot, followed by Raul Garcia on the twenty-second. All of them survived, although some will deal with damage both psychological and physical for the rest of their lives.

July 30, was the day that 22-year-old Robin Blasnek was shot and killed with the sawed-off shotgun while walking from her parents' home to her boyfriend's house. This would be the last murder by the Serial Street Shooters, and the one that Dieteman would tell a friend about. His confession led to the apprehension and arrest of himself and Dale Hausner.

The Killers

Samuel Dieteman was quite familiar with crime, and the police were quite familiar with him. He'd had over forty run-ins with the law, and his rap sheet contained arrests for driving while intoxicated, theft, possession of stolen property, assault, and child support delinquency. He was a wanted man in Minnesota at the time of the Arizona Serial Street Shooter case.

Dieteman said that he met Jeff and Dale Hausner in a Glendale bar in May of 2005. The three became friends. Dieteman had recently lost his job and been kicked out of his mother's house. He was becoming prolific at committing small thefts, setting fires, and assaulting people he came across.

After he began hanging out with the brothers, they would get high on meth, drink, and drive around causing trouble. Often they would hit stores like Wal-Mart and Target, stealing DVDs, alcohol, and whatever else they could.

Then the brothers started shooting animals from the car window, and one night they used a pellet gun to shoot a pedestrian. On their next foray they would use a higher caliber weapon, the .22 rifle, with devastating results.

Dale Hausner opened his home to Dieteman in July of 2005, allowing him to stay there with himself and his 2-year-old daughter Rebecca after Jeff had to downgrade into a smaller apartment. According to those who knew him, Hausner was a very different man before Dieteman's arrival. His neighbors saw him as shy, timid, and friendly.

Hausner had had two other children, boys ages two and three. They had been riding in the car with him while his wife drove when she fell asleep at the wheel and crashed into a creek. Both boys drowned. Rebecca was his daughter with another woman. He had custody of his little girl and seemed to live a quiet and simple life.

After Dieteman moved in, the people around Hausner said he began to change. He no longer greeted or returned the greetings of neighbors. He became withdrawn and socially awkward, uncomfortable to be around. Some said he seemed to become darker.

What his neighbors did not know was that Dale Hausner already had a bit of a dark streak. One of his ex-wives would testify that he had held her at gunpoint, threatening to shoot her. During the Serial Street Shooters investigation, it was revealed that Hausner was obsessed with a killer named Charles Starkweather, a teenager from Nebraska who had murdered eleven people back in 1958.

Throughout the crimes of the Baseline Killer and the Serial Street Shooters, Hausner collected every piece of newspaper that he could on the cases, the victims, and anything mentioning the murders. When police raided his apartment, they found scrapbooks and piles of clippings and articles about the cases.

Although Dieteman was the one with an extensive rap sheet, the Hausner brothers seem to have begun their own life of crime before Dieteman joined them. Their habit of drinking and smoking meth apparently prompted them to go on destructive jaunts through town. Robbery and petty theft were commonplace, and according to Dieteman, they had already committed some of the murders by the time he began riding with them on their nightly tours of terror.

Dale Hausner was known to take "orders" from people at his workplace—alcohol, DVDs, CDs, and other items he could later steal at supermarkets and other stores. The men set fire to trees, garbage cans, and a few stores later on. They shot animals, windows of businesses, and people.

In the wiretap transcripts, they laugh about various reactions and the dying words of their victims. They talk about the best technique for getting a good shot off, compliment each other on their shooting abilities, and fantasize about future victims.

Their goal was chaos, crimes without reason. The meth kept them awake, irrational, and impulsive. Alcohol further fueled their moods and carelessness. Although Dieteman would later claim that he purposefully missed his shots so as not to kill anyone, he was still a participant in the acts that filled the hearts and minds of the people of Phoenix with fear.

It was Dieteman's drinking habit that eventually led to their downfall. The Arizona police were already looking for Dieteman due to his alleged involvement in two different arson cases at two different Wal-Marts. At the time, they knew nothing about Dale Hausner. His brother Jeff, though, was known the Phoenix Police Department as a suspect in several stabbings. And when Dieteman spilled his secrets to a friend at a bar, the three men were done with their life of crime.

The Investigation

Samuel Dieteman spent most of his time at the Star Dust Inn bar. One of the friends he frequently drank with was Ron Horton.

By this point, authorities in Phoenix had become desperate. Billboards announced a $100,000 reward through the Silent Witness Hotline for any information leading to the capture and arrest of the Baseline Killer or the Serial Street Shooter(s).

So when Dieteman became intoxicated and morose and told Horton about some of the murders, Ron Horton felt burdened with the information. When Robin Blasnek was killed, he felt guilt, as his coming forward could possibly have prevented her murder. He called the hotline.

Looking at Dieteman's rap sheet, and discovering that he knew Jeff Hausner (with whom they were also familiar), investigators were sure they had a viable lead. Horton gave them Dieteman's cellphone number, which they traced, and told them Jeff Hausner's address, which they put under surveillance.

Investigators then asked Horton to meet with Dieteman at the bar. Undercover detectives sat around the establishment to monitor their conversation.

Dieteman arrived in a car with plates registered to Dale Hausner. The police weren't familiar with Dale, but the car matched the description of the light tan vehicle witnesses had described at the crime scenes.

Hausner dropped off Dieteman and left, so the police followed behind. Hausner drove to a nearby mall, where officers had a chance to place a GPS tracking device on his vehicle.

After a while, Horton took Dieteman to a hotel and casino and left him there for Hausner to pick up. Hausner and Dieteman spent some time in the casino before going back out to the car—where the officers watching saw them remove a long bag that looked like a rifle case from the trunk.

Rather than heading straight home, the two drove toward another residential area where they drove slowly through the streets, seeming to have no destination in mind. Police realized the two were hunting, looking for another victim.

Officers would later tell journalists about the fear and anxiety they felt as they followed the two around. "We were hoping and praying to God they wouldn't shoot anybody," one Detective Schwartzkopf said.

Using multiple "tail" cars, the investigators took turns following the killers and driving around telling anyone they saw to get off the streets as fast as they could. After an hour and a half, the duo went home.

After witnessing the killers on the prowl, the police were in a hurry to get them under arrest and safely away from society as quickly as possible. They received approval for an emergency wiretap. From the apartment next to Hausner's, they tapped his home.

"The sun was starting to go down, and I did not want to take that chance of another loss of life," one Detective Thomas later testified in court when the legality of the wiretap was challenged.

Below is a partial transcript of the wiretapped conversation between Hausner and Dieteman on September 3, 2006. It is recorded by the Phoenix Police Department as Case Number 2006 61281530 and transcribed by Detective Jason Buscher.

Hausner: ...have a lot of catching up to do.

Dieteman: The interview of the guys from the ATF office... (unintelligible)... plus the agents that worked in Washington D.C. on those two snipers there, they're a lot more experienced than us and had the... more technology and friggin' know-how even, since they worked on the case with the friggin' D.C. snipers... Here is the other one... Police just released this new bit of information that the sniper or serial shooter may circle around the area a couple of times to make sure there's no witnesses... ya think...?

Hausner: Ya think? Ya dumb motherfucker! It took them a year and half to come up with that? Wow!

Dieteman: In their face.

Hausner: ...You know that guy that got hit? So when'd you hear this stuff about the (stuttering) D.C. sniper stuff? Today?

Dieteman: Yeah, it was, uh, the five o'clock, four thirty or five o'clock, one of the two.

Hausner: Told you we'd love it. (grunts, unintelligible)

Dieteman: Hmm. (grunts, giggles, unintelligible)

Hausner: What are you looking at there? (high pitched noises and grunts) ...the American dollar... (unintelligible)... Look at this change over here. I don't... (unintelligible)... It was him? Oh my God!

Dieteman: On the five a.m. news, it was when they first said… Phoenix and Mesa Police have now officially linked (stutters) the shoo… shooting death of a young Mesa woman to the serial killer, which now brings the total to six.

Hausner: It's higher than that! What about the guy I fucking shot on 27th Avenue in the yard… (unintelligible)

Dieteman: Working with the feds and other states because they believe that these people, they don't… may have begun in another state… are looking for similar crimes in other states.

Hausner: Really?

Dieteman: (unintelligible)

Hausner: Hmm, so we're being copycatted, Sam? We're pioneers, Sam? We're leading the way for a better life for everybody, Sam?

Dieteman: I guess it started in another state and… (unintelligible)… finish it.

Hausner: You know how they got that, uh… they think that they circle around? They probably saw my car in that fucking… fuckin' surveillance camera about three times.

Dieteman: I'm gonna get some of that tanning stuff. Figure, black hair. If I can dye the rest of my facial hair black and then tan real well… (unintelligible)… they'll think I'm a Hispanic guy.

Hausner: I got shot by a Hispanic guy, man.

Dieteman: Put a yellow hat on.

Dieteman: …head, though. It kept soaking right down to my skin so I just washed it off.

Hausner: …watching anybody fight like that. Wait, hold on. It's time to give Sam a hug night-night…

Dieteman: I want to give Becky a hug.

Hausner: Becky, give him a hug night-night.

Dieteman: Nah, she ain't gonna hug me.

Hausner: Give Sam a hug. Aww, isn't that nice.

Dieteman: Aww…

Hausner: Say "Goodnight, Sam."

Rebecca: Goodnight, Sam.

Dieteman: Night-night, Becky.

Hausner: See you in the morning.

Rebecca: See you in the morning.

Hausner: Say "Don't kill anybody."

Dieteman: In the morning? That's too early.

Rebecca: …it's too early.

Hausner: Say "Don't kill anybody."

Rebecca: Don't kill anybody.

Dieteman: Oh, alright. Since you asked.

Rebecca: (babbles)

Hausner: Five more minutes and we're gonna go to bed. Say "Bye, Sam, be careful."

Hausner: This fuckin' guy—no, it's not two guys—are better than the Baseline rapist.

Dieteman: (laughing, unintelligible)

Hausner: One's got a gun and one's got a condom. (laughs)

Dieteman: One prophylactic, semi-used. (laughs)

Hausner: Really, he's a maniac?

Dieteman: (metallic sound) Damn it.

Hausner: What?

Dieteman: Here what I have… I'm getting me another obituary.

Hausner: It'll be in both the Mesa and *The Arizona Republic*… (unintelligible)

Dieteman: No, I mean I'm not worried about getting my own. I'm getting another one.

Hausner: She was shot. Where we shot that bitch? Fuckin' cunt! They shot her and when people looked that way, "Ugh," they ran out. She was on her knees, "Oh, I've been shot," blood po... pouring out, right? (higher voice pitch) "Oh my God!" A rag or a towel is not gonna cut it and not a blanket, you know. She goes, "I've been shot!"

Dieteman: (laughing)

(voices overlap, laughing)

Dieteman: Oh my God! She looks familiar from somewhere! You know a Blasnek?

Hausner: Um... I don't think so.

Dieteman: Hmm... for some reason looks kinda familiar...

Hausner: I know a "Blast-neck."

Dieteman: Hmm... here's a Samuel.

Hausner: Are you ready? There Angels don't fear the path they tread. We got to do them next, man.

Dieteman: Something firing, something loud, the caller told 911 operator. Mesa police won't say where on the victim was hit. Why don't you say on her leg, dumb motherfucker… she said there were no witnesses in the Mesa shootings and the surviving victim hasn't provided information to police that points to a suspect. Phoenix Police spokesman, our buddy Andy Hill, told reporters involved that we don't want to deter tips to police and aren't releasing profiles of who the criminals might be. God, I wish I would have seen that news thing were they had that psychic. That would have been prime. This is just speculation, but the two may be competing with each other. (laughs)

Hausner: What do you think that motherfucker's sitting around doing? That motherfucker steal my motherfucking thunder!

Dieteman: Motherfucker! (unintelligible)

Hausner: A picture of that in here, that be… (unintelligible)… wouldn't it?

Dieteman: It's horrible.

Hausner: It's horrible. You… schlep…

Dieteman: So I called Brodie Broderson, a 22-year veteran… was even issued a red beret… (whispering) cause you're a queer.

Hausner: I want to shoot 'em and take a red beret.

Dieteman: Do I have to wear that hat she asked?… I want to shoot somebody with one of them berets on, I mean, while wearing one.

(voices unintelligible)

Dieteman: No, I mean I want one on my head while I'm shooting. So if there is somebody like down the road that sees it, "He was wearing a red beret. Shot by an Angel."

Hausner: An Angel. (coughs/laughs)

Dieteman: Red beret... army surplus store or something. They got to have some kind of red beret.

Hausner: Get one and dye one. Die die die die, bitches!

(News in background about cases.)

Dieteman: 23 violent crimes? I thought there was 27 altogether.

Hausner: ...(unintelligible)... Add it up! Add it up!

(News mentions $100,000 for information on the Serial Shooter or Baseline Killer.)

Dieteman: 27, it's still 35... actually 36.

Hausner: Serial Shooter information. What or who is the Serial Shooter? A person who is believed to be responsible for 36 street shootings since May '05. Five people have been killed and 16 wounded. How do we know that all of the shootings were by one person and not copycats? They are primarily located... by similarities, including time... blah, blah, blah. Where are the shootings occurring? They're always on major streets... (seems to be reading the newspaper) The fatal shooting on Sunday night was not on a major street. Bullshit! Fuckin' people, fuckin' Gilbert's not a major street?

Dieteman: Gilbert's not a major street? Really?

Hausner: Fucking... from fucking Mesa to Tempe to fucking Gilbert...

Dieteman: Not a major street?

Hausner: I'm sorry, Mesa to fucking Gilbert to Chandler... that's not a major street. Oh, okay, fucking cunt!

Dieteman: I wish I was fuckin' somewhere close to where one of them fuckin' red beret pricks, the Guardian Angels, and walk up there say, you know...

Hausner: I love you.

Dieteman: No, stay up here, you know... sweet talk... and bust out the knife hook. Ahh! (Screams and laughs)

Hausner: (laughs)

Dieteman: It would just be freakin' cooler than shit, though... here is an Angel found stabbed to death.

Hausner: ...(unintelligible)...

Dieteman: Oh, that would be great... I had a feeling I was gonna miss. I'm looking up, once you pointed him out, I came in and then I looked up and that freakin' stupid helicopter... I don't know why I'm so paranoid about that, and I'm looking back, and lookin' this way, and by the time we're up there and I cock it and started bringing it up and that fucker... almost on top of me...

Hausner: What was the shooter's motive? Can't provide detail. How close was the shooter to the victims? Can't provide detail. Is it legal to carry a Taser for protection? You can carry a Taser, but not concealed. Is it possible the shooter fired from behind a bush or tree? Possible... Police are working with a task force that includes federal agencies... Have you ruled out gangland initiation as a motive? We're looking at everything.

Dieteman: Everything?

Hausner: It's the 9th Street gang, fuckin' Carbajal.

Dieteman: Vatos, locos, cabron, ghetto, bitches.

Hausner: It's a new...

Dieteman: I love you...

Hausner: It's a new fear gang called The Act of I Love You.

Dieteman: Ha-ha-ha... Oh fuck, imagine that hitting the TV.

Dieteman: (laughing) We believe this to be... be an African national. His name is Mmph-ah-mm-tah... (unintelligible)

Hausner: I'm dead, pack my mud.

Dieteman: (laughing) Pack my mud. Maybe you're using his porn star name of "Mud Packer." I'm dead, pack my mud.

Hausner: I'm deadious, pack my mudious…his nickname is Mudious Packious Deadious… shootious in the backious. I love shooting people in the back. (laughing) It's so much fun.

Dieteman: It is.

Hausner: Yeah. (laughing) That fucking old man I shot in the back. "Ah!" Shit all over the place. "My mud!"

Dieteman: My favorite thing is, you know, when somebody is walking away, you know. It gives me, you know, an extra couple of seconds to aim. I don't have to worry about them looking. I get too paranoid of somebody walking toward me and while I'm trying to aim that they're frickin' gonna see me, or not… not so much see me but see the gun stickin' out wrong or somethin'… and be able to give a description. That's why I think I try to wait till the last second when somebody's coming towards me and… (unintelligible)… Normally, I don't even get it to my eye, I just get it somewhere where it looks like the barrel's pointed toward them and then bang!

Hausner: See, how I do it, though…

Dieteman: You're fucking quick with it! You just frickin' get up there and get your bead right on them, bam!

Hausner: Bam! (screams) Quick… hang gun… (slapping sound)

Dieteman: Speaking of… 12 gauge with some kind of thing on the end. That big 'ol shell in there. When I'm in the freakin' back seat of the car, window down, already up to the shoulder, already a bead on somebody. Just as soon as it comes right where, uh… the separation between the window roller all of a sudden, then the barrel protrudes from the window with… (unintelligible) and bam!

Dieteman: If you happen to come upon a... weapon. I wanna get that .38 if that bitch Marin would sell it. I don't know if she knows that shit's in her car. I'm pretty sure she does.

Hausner: Do you know... do... (stutters) do you know where she lives?

Dieteman: Nah.

Hausner: Do you know where she works?

Dieteman: In a Dave's... bar or something. I can find out from somebody where she works. There's that frickin two of my knives. One that I use, one that... (unintelligible)... We need to get that .38 friggin revolver which could be used on a couple of people. I got so pissed at him for not getting rid of that shit. He's all, "Come on, it's perfectly fine." What's it hidden for? Let me use it. Like, no. It would be great because I'm not as paranoid as I used to be. I want the fucking revolver. A little .38 would be great, you know, somebody just would walk up.

Hausner: You could walk around town.

Dieteman: You could just walk up, you know, and be like, "Hi," you know, and who the fuck are you? Some jangy ass bum or something. "Hey, I got some money."

Hausner: Hey man, you got some motherfuckin' change, motherfucker...

Dieteman: I'll be like, yeah, here, let me get my wallet out, and then I get my wallet in this hand I got the .38 there. Right here, motherfucker.

Hausner: Hey!

Dieteman: Boom! Then I get a chance to watch 'em just fall.

Hausner: Yeah. (laughing) You got the motherfuckin' snatch for a nigga, brother.

Dieteman: (laughs) Snatch.

Hausner: (laughs) That's what they say.

Dieteman: That's a motherfucker...

Hausner: That's a motherfucker black for ya.

Dieteman: That's a broke motherfucker. Yankee-ass, yo.

Hausner: Yeah!

Dieteman: (unintelligible) Yankee-ass motherfuck! Pow, pow, pow, powerful.

Hausner: (unintelligible)

Dieteman: (laughs) Motherfucker, right? Fuckin' niggy... boy.

Hausner: Yeah, yeah!

Dieteman: Just watch him on the (unintelligible) for me.

Hausner: You pull it out and pow, pow, pow, pow!

Dieteman: Yeah, I know, right in the fuckin' head or something. Right by an eyeball or something. Forehead.

Hausner: (unintelligible)

Dieteman: Watch him just... backwards.

Hausner: (unintelligible) Sorry...

Investigators were in disbelief. Hausner and Dieteman were almost constantly watching the news—with the exception of a time period when *The Jungle Book* was playing in the background—or reading it in the newspaper. Fueled by alcohol and methamphetamine, they mocked the investigation, the statements, and their victims. They discussed the Baseline Killer and compared him to themselves. They also discussed details of several of the crimes that had not been revealed to the public. That was all the police would need to arrest the two and obtain a warrant to search the apartment for evidence.

Fearing for the safety of the child inside, they opted to wait for the men to come out rather than raiding the apartment.

That evening, Dieteman exited carrying the garbage out to the dumpsters. Police in SWAT gear approached and he immediately dropped the bag and surrendered. The bag was later found to contain shotgun shells and a map with the murders marked on it. Dieteman handed the officers the key to the apartment, and they went in to confront Hausner.

As they entered, Hausner had his back turned. When they announced their presence he was startled but compliant. The successful apprehension of the Serial Street Shooters came on August 3, 2006, nearly a year after they had begun their crime spree.

Hausner denied everything, but Dieteman immediately began to talk. Unlike the Baseline Killer, he had no qualms about confessing to murder.

Hausner had miscellaneous "alibis" for some of the murders. He kept them in a notebook that he used to keep track of the lies he told the various women he was seeing. Unfortunately for Hausner, his notebook was thoroughly discredited when the women testified against his statements.

Nevertheless, many people who knew Hausner were baffled by his arrest. He had a dual personality. In one he was a heartbroken and loving father, a friendly neighbor and good employee. In the other, he was a thief, a meth user, an alcoholic, and a self-centered man who saw no repercussions to what he did.

Based on evidence, Dale Hausner was the main suspect. Samuel Dieteman's statements bolstered the evidence and detailed his own part in the crimes. As Michael Kiefer, a reporter for *The Arizona Republic*, wrote:

Dieteman let it all spill out the day he was arrested. He and Dale Hausner, he told police, were engaged in what they called "random, recreational violence".

There were muggings, stabbings, palm trees torched, stores set on fire, tires slashed. And the shootings. Essentially they were playing video games in real life while smoking meth.

"Everything they did was about creating havoc," Phoenix Police Detective Schwartzkopf said.

Once they even shot a man, then parked the car and went to look at the damage they had done. Police were already on the scene. They questioned Dieteman and Dale Hausner, who gave their names and made-up stories about what they had seen and heard. Then the officers let them go.

The vehicle registered to Hausner was familiar to the witnesses. Surveillance footage put Hausner at or near some crime scenes. The men's wiretapped conversation was even more damning.

The Trial

The trials of Samuel Dieteman and Dale Hausner were very different affairs. Dieteman held nothing back, while Hausner used deflection and lies to try to prove his innocence. As witness testimonies piled up, they bolstered Dieteman's timeline of events and suggested that he was being honest in his statements. The evidence left little doubt as to the guilt of either man, and Hausner, albeit refusing to plead guilty, eventually begged for death.

Hausner's trial was first. Despite his refusal to admit guilt, he also refused some of his attorneys' requests to use his difficult childhood and the loss of his sons as part of his defense. Instead, Hausner produced the notebook full of female names and entries recording the stories he had told each woman. As much as people thought him shy, Hausner's attorney, Tim Agan, stated that Hausner was a ladies' man. Hausner had apparently written the notebook specifically to provide himself with alibis for many of the crimes. The ladies in question, though, weren't willing to jump on board with his lies. Each one who took the witness stand quickly denied each alibi he had constructed.

When his declarations of innocence weren't enough, Hausner began to theorize about the crimes himself. He told the court that Dieteman must have been using his vehicle and weapon, sneaking out at night to commit the crimes. He also discussed his brother's involvement, more so than Dieteman had.

However, there was no denying his image on surveillance footage from near the crime scenes, his own words on tape, or the witness statements, not to mention the stories from his co-conspirator, Samuel Dieteman. As the trial progressed, Hausner requested that his attorneys not fight the death penalty.

Despite not pleading guilty, he showed remorse to the victims' families and said that they deserved closure for what had happened to their relatives. There is a possibility this remorse stemmed not only from his feelings of guilt, but from depression about the loss of his two sons. He knew firsthand the pain and loss that the families had suffered.

Hausner faced 87 charges covering arsons, destruction of property, robberies, assaults, firearms violations, and eight murders. On six of those eight murders, and 80 out of the 87 charges, Hausner was convicted.

While waiting for his sentence, Hausner spoke to the families, the jury, and others in the courtroom. While he did feel remorse and said he was sorry for what happened to the victims, he also brought out his fascination with serial killers. He compared himself to Charles Manson and even stated that later on, his name would be as infamous. He knew that he was forever tainted by the murders.

With the murder convictions, Hausner was up for the death penalty. Since he had requested his attorneys not to fight it, they didn't. After the jurors came back with the sentence, satisfying Hausner's request and granting him the death penalty, Hausner thanked them. One of the jurors told him "you're welcome" as he left.

Jeff Hausner stood trial next. Unfortunately, there was insufficient evidence to convict him of any of the Serial Street Shooters crimes. However, due to Dieteman's testimony, he was indicted for attempted murder in a stabbing incident. He was already in prison serving a seven-and-a-half-year sentence for another stabbing when the jury found him guilty, adding 18 years to his current sentence.

Dieteman was sentenced in July of 2012. Thanks to his cooperation and testimony against Dale Hausner, the jury gave him life without the possibility of parole.

Dale Hausner, although he'd received the sentence he asked for, was not entirely satisfied. Frustrated at how long it would take to be executed, he went as far as to try to waive all further appeals to move the process along.

In situations where a convict wants the death penalty, there is often a concern that he is mentally unstable. When Arizona authorities began to question Hausner's mental health, Hausner had something to say to that:

"The state of Arizona wanted me to get the death penalty before and during my trial," he wrote. "I was found guilty and given six death sentences. Now that I want to get executed, suddenly my mental state is in question. So, if I am found incompetent to waive my appeals, does that mean I was also incompetent to stand trial? That's something to think about, isn't it? I am not insane. I am of sound mind. I simply wish to get the punishment handed down to me, but more quickly. I mean, really, what's a guy got to do to get snuffed out?"

A year later, in July of 2013, Dale Hausner was found unconscious in his cell. He died at the hospital later that day. It was discovered that he had taken an intentional overdose of the drug Elavil, or amitriptyline. He had found a way to "get snuffed out" on his own terms.

Psychological Imbalance

The Serial Street Shooters had a similar dynamic to most serial killing duos: There is an alpha personality and a weaker, more subservient personality that goes along with the former. In this case, Dale Hausner (and to some extent his brother Jeff) was the stronger of the two, with Samuel Dieteman being a wayward criminal who got in too deep.

As with the Baseline Killer, drugs and alcohol played a major part in their activities and the extent of the crimes they committed. But of course there are many people addicted to the same substances who aren't roaming around killing people.

Unlike the Baseline Killer, the Serial Street Shooters felt remorse for what they did, but they refused to accept the full weight of blame for their crimes.

Dale Hausner was a racist and an angry man. Prior to the killings, Hausner had engaged in bouts of violence towards the people closest to him, such as his ex-wife. He had delusions of grandeur, a skewed perception of reality, and issues with impulse control. Fueled by his constant use of alcohol and methamphetamine, he became a truly monstrous entity.

There is one momentous event that undoubtedly explain some of Hausner's personality issues: the deaths of his sons. Dale Hausner was a passenger in the car his wife was driving when she fell asleep and drove into a creek. Both of his young sons perished. Hausner claimed that he had tried to rescue them but was unable to.

The young daughter living with him at the time of the murders was sickly and had to be fed via a tube in her stomach. However, there was absolutely no indication that she was harmed or mistreated by Hausner. This shows that he had an ability to feel significant compassion and love for his children. It is thus possible that the death of his sons was a trigger that took the substance abuse and anger to another level. There are no clear signs that he displayed any extreme behavior beforehand.

Then again, his ex-wife Karen, the mother of the two deceased sons, said that Hausner was not the man people thought he was. She related a relationship of abuse and threats on her own life. At one point, she told reporters, Hausner made her get in the car and drove her out to the desert. He pulled out a shotgun and claimed it was the weapon he would eventually kill her with.

If Karen was being honest about Hausner's darker side, it raises questions as to what happened when their sons died. Was Hausner asleep as well? Did he do something to make her crash? As with Mark Goudeau's wife, Wendy Carr, there is the possibility that Karen suffered from battered woman syndrome and protected him at the time. It must be noted, though, that is merely speculation on the part of some journalists.

Whether or not he was truly the loving and caring father everyone saw is hard to say. Neighbors around his apartment said that the big changes in him occurred only after Samuel Dieteman moved in. None of the neighbors liked Dieteman, and many said that they felt wary of his presence.

Jeff Hausner also had some influence on his brother. With a history of assault and substance abuse and a subsequent arrest and conviction for stabbing someone, he was possibly the influence for Dale Hausner to take a more violent approach.

This is where the methamphetamine use becomes a huge factor. Meth is a drug often used by lower-income drug abusers. It is made with ingredients that can be purchased at any store and is often readily available in the shadier areas of poor neighborhoods. Meth is instantly addictive and has a severe effect on the brain. Some of the long-term effects of meth use include violent tendencies, paranoia, and anxiety. This, coupled with the loss of sleep and appetite, often leads a habitual meth user to act irrationally and impulsively. They steal, they react violently, they lie, they manipulate, and their only goal is to achieve their next high. Meth can also give them a false sense of near immortality and an unshakable feeling of being in control when they are very clearly not.

The bulk of Hausner's behavior can be attributed to the unhealthy coping mechanisms he used to deal with the death of his children. He had lost respect for people because they had died at the hands of someone he loved and trusted. The use of alcohol and meth to escape his pain heightened his issues with petty crime and accelerated his progression to murder.

He originally denied being involved in the killings, and even tried to place the blame on his brother. Often, though, Dale Hausner would slip up. He had a fascination with serial killers. Charles Starkweather was one he often talked about and even collected information on. He was in awe of Charles Manson. He'd saved every newspaper and magazine article mentioning the serial killings in Phoenix. His secret obsession was not so secret by the time of the trial, and it certainly did not support his Not Guilty plea. Even though he claimed to be innocent, he asked his lawyers not to fight the death penalty.

Hausner's request to be executed led to a mental evaluation which concluded that he was severely depressed and remorseful and showed signs of suicidal tendencies. He was placed on antidepressants shortly after his sentencing. His final murder was that of himself, via an intentional overdose of his medications.

Samuel Dieteman was a different story. Dieteman was a hardened criminal long before he met Hausner. Drugs, alcohol, and a life of petty crime were already commonplace for him.

Dieteman was also quick to talk once he was arrested. He admitted to the murder he committed and another he was involved in. He told authorities that he had intentionally shot to wound after the first murder, so that he could placate his co-conspirator. He feigned bad aim in order to save lives—or so he said. The fact that the rest of his victims survived his shotgun blasts does support his claim that his intention was to wound rather than kill, though.

Dieteman presented himself as somewhat of a victim, a man who went along with a murderer out of fear for his life. The problem with this stance is that Dieteman was the one with the crime issues. He was well known to Phoenix law enforcement authorities as a thief, arsonist, meth addict, alcoholic, and all-around petty criminal. He didn't have the connection with his children that Hausner did, and he was even wanted on a warrant for child support delinquency. Whereas Hausner at least outwardly appeared to be a likable and a decent man, Dieteman was the opposite. And yet, despite this, according to Dieteman and some of the evidence, it was actually Hausner who was the violent criminal leader and Dieteman the meek tagalong.

Dieteman's needs were his primary motivation for participation in the crimes. He needed a place to stay, he needed financial help after losing his job, he needed alcohol and meth to feed his addictions, and he needed friends that he felt he could trust. Once again, addiction played a major part in the story. The petty crimes of his past rolled over as he began to get involved in the same types of crimes with the Hausner brothers.

Violent criminal behavior has been linked to methamphetamine use in a study by Stretesky (2009) indicating that even after adjusting for demographic characteristics and use of other substances including alcohol, heroin and crack/cocaine, the odds of committing a homicide are nearly nine times greater for those who use methamphetamine compared to those who do not.

However, the association of methamphetamine use and violence is neither consistent nor unidirectional in apparent causation and appears conditional on many personal and contextual characteristics (Tyner & Fremouw, 2008). Sommers & Baskin (2006) suggest methamphetamine-related violence may stem from the interaction of the individual, the substance, and the situation, as methamphetamine use provides several mechanisms for motivating violence, including inhibition of cues that normally control behavior, increased arousal, interference with interpersonal communication, and intensification of emotions.

Violent criminal behaviors are more likely to be reported among males, younger respondents, those with an early history of physical abuse, with each of the psychological comorbidity indicators, or by those who use more types of drugs as well as specific drugs (crack, inhalants, PCP, and opiates) or regularly use alcohol to intoxication. In addition, violent criminal behaviors are more often reported by those with greater methamphetamine addiction severity, more methamphetamine-related problems as well as some specific methamphetamine-related problems (violence, paranoia, hallucinations, skin problems, high blood pressure), those involved in methamphetamine sales or manufacture, or those with early arrests. (www.ncbi.nlm.nih.gov)

With most drug abusers, the overwhelming want and need for the drug eventually gets in the driver's seat and takes a spin of its own. Methamphetamine, in particular, is known to be almost immediately addictive. Many users state that once the drug is in their system, they feel increasingly nauseous, lethargic, and overall ill the longer they go without it. Once they take it, though, their heart and mind begin racing, and yet their thought processes are slowed. They have to do something, anything, but they aren't thinking clearly enough to do anything productive or perform their exploits safely. Many end up turning to crime or violence, and almost all make bad decisions and do things no normal, logical person would do. They are trying to get their minds and bodies caught up with their racing hearts and chemical-induced confusion. Thus the comedown isn't just psychological; they feel physically drained, like a coffee person in the morning before their first cup. How do they get going again? More drugs.

The Acadian Addiction Center divides the effects of methamphetamine into several categories. Mood symptoms include euphoria, overall sense of wellbeing, depression, and anxiety. Behavioral symptoms include mounting legal problems, preoccupation with obtaining, using, and recovering from methamphetamine use, social isolation, hiding drug use from others, dangerous, risky behaviors, impulsiveness, unexplained financial problems, incarceration, interpersonal relationship problems, violent behaviors, appetite depression, binge/crash pattern of abuse, aggression, risky sexual behaviors, and "tweaking"—intently-focused attention. Physical symptoms include trembling and shaking, nausea and vomiting, insomnia, tolerance, addiction, "meth mouth", open sores, hair loss, loss of skin elasticity, decreased blood flow through the body's tissues, vasoconstriction, tachycardia, liver damage, and extreme rise in core temperature of body. Psychological symptoms include nervousness, repetitive behaviors, disorganized thoughts, hallucinations, "meth bugs" or the sensation of bugs crawling underneath the skin, and paranoia.

These symptoms may lead to effects such as homelessness, malnutrition, incarceration, financial ruin, divorce, domestic and child abuse, full-blown toxic psychosis, extreme paranoia, impotence, tooth loss, compulsive, obsessive behaviors—tweaking, alterations in memory and cognition, violent behaviors, functional changes in the brain, behavioral changes, brain damage, decline in reasoning, motor skills, and judgment, destruction of the body's tissues and blood vessels, inability for the body to properly repair damaged tissues, anhedonia—the inability to feel pleasure, increased infectious diseases, seizures, coma, heart attack, stroke, and death.

The withdrawal symptoms are also rather telling. They include deep, dark depression, decreased energy, increased sleeping, teeth grinding, night sweats, emotional labiality, irritability, resumption of eating, leading to weight gain, anxiety, craving methamphetamines, anhedonia, suicidal ideations, and suicide.

Note that Dale Hausner became severely depressed and suicidal after his arrest. Considering his inability to use meth while in prison, it is reasonable to assume that withdrawal from the drug could have had more bearing on his sense of remorse than any actual guilt.

Although drug abuse can cause many issues, there are many people addicted to drugs such as meth and cocaine who do not become serial killers. The predilection for violence involving the sequential murders of other people comes from a multitude of issues within the person, or persons.

In the case of the Serial Street Shooters, there is also the possibility of a mob mentality on top of the plethora of psychological issues and drug abuse. Dieteman may have felt the need to go on with the crimes in order to stay in Dale Hausner's good graces. Likewise, Dale committed his original crimes with his brother Jeff, another drug user, alcoholic and petty criminal; he could have been influenced to escalate his crimes so as to seem "cool" or "badass" as his brother. However, there isn't enough public information on Jeff Hausner to get a read on how his personality might have affected the other two.

Again, though, even if no one of them bore sole responsibility for the killings, none of the men experienced enough remorse or guilt during their spree to stop or to go to the police. Honor, pride, or enjoyment of the crimes themselves could all be reasons why they continued to kill.

In truth, until more information is released about the psychological evaluations done by the courts, it is hard to say what exactly prompted these men to go from petty crimes and domestic disturbances to serial killings. Well-known early warning signs of a serial killer include late-age bed-wetting, arson and fascination with fires, and injuring, torturing, and killing animals. These behaviors are admittedly rather crude indicators without much predictive value, as they can easily result from other mental issues or life circumstances. Even so, it is worth noting that the Serial Street Shooters did begin their crime spree with arsons and animal killings.

Part III: The Aftermath

Phoenix Reeling

The killers had been apprehended, tried, and sentenced, but Phoenix was left shaken.

The Phoenix Police Department, especially, seemed like it could not get a break. The family of Romelia Vargas sued the department for millions of dollars, besmirching its professionalism and alleging that police officials had been busier seeking a claim to fame rather than the killer. Meanwhile, Mark Goudeau's wife rallied a segment of the community against the department by alleging racial discrimination and trying to discredit the evidence against her husband.

Initially, the police were simply relieved they had captured the serial killers and ended the terrifying rampage of the Serial Street Shooters and the Baseline Killer. But then information about the investigation itself began to come out—and this demonstrated how negligence and failure to follow available leads and evidence had allowed the Baseline Killer to murder people who would still be alive if he had been arrested on the DNA evidence of an earlier case.

This claim was put forward most vigorously by the family of Romelia Vargas in a multimillion-dollar lawsuit. Their official complaint recited their identities, described how Romelia supported her large family, and listed evidence that had allegedly been neglected. Halfway through, it stated:

The factual foundation for this claim is the intentional, reckless and grossly negligent conduct by members of the Phoenix Police Department and the Phoenix Crime Laboratory that directly lead to Romelia's murder on February 20, 2006. The perpetrator of this crime is Goudeau, deemed the "Baseline Killer" by the local press. Romelia is but one of Goudeau's many victims, and had the Phoenix Police Department and its crime lab outsourced DNA testing to DPS in a timely and reasonable manner, not only would her murder not have happened, but several other tragedies would have been avoided as well.

Throughout the fall of 2005 and for the next year thereafter, Goudeau committed a series of violent crimes on random members of the public. Goudeau committed 9 murders and 15 sexual assaults in at least 16 different violent crimes.

The Phoenix Police Department gathered 2 separate DNA samples from a victim of a sexual assault in September 2005. This evidence was from the perpetrator of the crime. Had this evidence been timely studied, the results would have ended Goudeau's crime spree. Phoenix had reason to believe that the series of violent crimes was being committed by one person before February of 2006. However, this evidence was not subjected to testing until summer of 2006, approximately 1 year and 9 murders later.

Claimants believe the evidence will show that members of the Phoenix Police Department, including those acting in a supervisory capacity as well as managers, purposefully decided not to test the above described DNA samples for reasons having nothing to do with reasonable police practices and procedures. They were motivated by public relations and interagency competition. Simply put, members of the Phoenix Police Department and Phoenix crime lab wanted credit for solving the crimes. This decision not to test was an intentional act and outrageous in nature.

In the alternative, the decision not to test the DNA sample was reckless or grossly negligent, as the members of the Police Department and Phoenix crime lab knew and understood the alternative to not testing the DNA samples was that further violent crimes would lead to more injured victims and grieving families. As the number of sexual assaults and murders grew during the remainder of 2005 and continued growing well into 2006, the callousness of the decision not to test the DNA became obscene.

There is no question about the effect of testing the DNA sample. The DNA test DPS conducted immediately led to the arrest of the perpetrator of the sexual assaults and murders, including Romelia's murder. The arrest was a direct result of the testing without any discussion or professional decision as to whether the owner of the DNA should or should not have been arrested.

It is clear and undisputed that as a direct and proximate result of the Phoenix Police Department's intentional, reckless and grossly negligent decision not to test the DNA, Romelia was murdered. But for the intentional, reckless and gross conduct of managers and supervisors at the Phoenix Police Department and the Phoenix Crime Laboratory, she would be alive today.

The complaint requested a total of 22 million dollars to be divided in specified amounts among Romelia's family members. It was filed about two years after Mark Goudeau's arrest and was based on information and statements from investigators who were working on or around the case. The investigators laid the blame on the incompetence of the Phoenix Crime Lab, whereas the claimants pointed a finger at the entire Phoenix Police Department.

In fact, the complaint made a number of allegations against specific members of the department. They included Chief of Police Jack Harris; Assistant Chief of Police Tracy Montgomery; Assistant Chief of Police Andy Anderson; Lieutenant Venny Pina; Crime Lab Commander Brett Vermeer; Crime Lab DNA Supervisor Roger Schneider; and Schneider's assistant Alison Sedowski. According to the complaint, these individuals failed to process the evidence for no good professional reason.

When the initial lawsuit failed, the family tried to sue the police department a second time. In the end, an appeals court ruled that crime victims' families could not sue police over the deaths of their loved ones. Azcentral, the website of *The Arizona Republic*, reported that "the state Court of Appeals ruling Thursday says the city didn't have a special duty to protect the victims and that a state immunity law otherwise blocks negligence claims stemming from the crimes that included nine killings."

Although that got the victims' families off the department's back, Mark Goudeau and his wife Wendy Carr were also going after the Phoenix Police Department with claims varying from racial discrimination to falsifying and planting evidence. They too failed to succeed in court, as many of the claims they made were contradicted by Mark Goudeau's own behavior, past and present. Also working against them was the unlikelihood that some of the evidence—such as the jewelry taken from victims' bodies that was found in Goudeau's home—could have been planted. Finally, some of Wendy Carr's statements did more to discredit her than help her husband. She said that he was constitutionally incapable of being violent or raping someone, when he had actually been convicted of those very offenses; and she said he had never used cocaine, which he had been found with, tested positive for, and admitted to taking.

All of the hoopla from the original cases had barely died down when the summer of 2015 came around and carried with it a serial shooter, a serial killer, and a host of small groups of copycat shooters. The shooters, luckily, didn't take any lives, but the serial killer was a different story.

It began when someone shot out the windows of a car. More cars began to take bullets, but no one was seriously injured. And then someone began shooting at people in their homes, near their homes, and on the streets—and not everyone survived these attacks.

It was 2015 and yet 2005 came flooding back. Within a month the I-10 shooter was apprehended, albeit after several failed leads on various suspects. Police then caught at least three copycat groups using pellet guns and slingshots to attack vehicles.

But the one shooting from the streets was still loose. It would take a year, until the summer of 2016, for the Phoenix Police Department to arrest Aaron Saucedo for the murders and assaults. The trials are still ongoing, with nine murders and three other assaults confirmed and more suspected.

Many people in Phoenix have been asking for transparency in the case of Aaron Saucedo, the Maryvale Serial Street Shooter. Many of the records are sealed, as part of the ongoing investigation. What journalists were able to recover about Saucedo showed that he fit many textbook expectations of a serial killer. Suacedo, 23 years old, has no criminal record albeit a traffic citation for running a red light whilst driving a city bus. Despite his young age, he had no social media presence or activities. Aaron Saucedo lived with his mother, was seen as rather quiet, and had no history of causing trouble or being a troubled kid. He did attend both public school and a school for "troubled youths," but the school specified that not only did they have juvenile delinquents, but also kids from poverty or difficult backgrounds. No one at his schools recalled him ever being in trouble or having any personality issues.

The first victim of Aarron Saucedo was a man who had been in a relationship with Saucedo's mother. He was shot and killed outside of his home with a 9mm pistol that Saucedo later pawned. It was the only victim with any ties to the killer. Witness descriptions led to a police sketch that looked very much like Saucedo. His dark colored BMW was also part of the statements given to police, although he stopped driving it and attempted to alter his appearance after the witness descriptions were released to the public. Aarron Saucedo was noted as a loner who kept himself in isolation with no known criminal record or mental issues. There is still no solid motive as to why he snapped and began killing people. He drove around in his car, much like the Phoenix Serial Street Shooters of 2005, picking out victims and shooting them. The prosecution is currently seeking the death penalty for his case.

With the public awaiting the outcome of the Saucedo case, Phoenix's past is encroaching back into the media. The sordid history of serial killers in Phoenix was never forgotten, but the uncanny coincidence of two different years, ten years apart, featuring such similar crimes has brought it back into the limelight. As Phoenix struggles with its daily crime issues, residents now have the world contemplating the seemingly high incidence of serial killers in their city.

At any given minute, there are many serial killers active all over the world. The exact number fluctuates from the 30s up to nearly 200. Many are not reported to the public. This is to prevent both panic and attempts at vigilante justice, as some may think they have the case figured out and go after the suspect they have identified.

What this means is that Phoenix may not have an unnaturally high rate of serial killings. The series of cases a decade apart may be mere coincidence.

On top of this, there is the issue of social media bringing stories to millions of people in a matter of seconds. News stories that would formerly remain in a small area now spread around the world at an unbelievable pace.

Many of the current articles on Phoenix's 2005-2006 serial killers speculate about how things might have been different if the internet was as accessible and interactive then as it is now. Although social media can generate fear and panic, it can also result in quicker action by the public. Information, police sketches, and surveillance camera images of the suspects could have spread faster. More people would have known about the killings, and some of them might have been able to identify the perpetrators or give other information to the police.

There are instances of criminals giving themselves away faster due to the internet as well. Dale Hausner and Samuel Dieteman searched for as much information as possible about their own crimes, and they loved talking about them to each other. What if their crimes occurred now? When the articles popped up on their newsfeed, could they resist the temptation to comment on them?

Currently, the serial killers of Phoenix, Arizona, are facing either a multitude of life sentences or the death penalty. For the time being, Phoenix is safe—at least from the Serial Street Shooters, the Baseline Killer, and Aaron Saucedo.

Timeline of Events

This is a timeline of the murders and attacks in Phoenix, Arizona, during the 2005-2006 serial killings.

- May 17, 2005 (Serial Street Shooters)—Tony Mendez (39) is shot and killed.
- May 24, 2005 (Serial Street Shooters)—Reginald Remillard (56) is shot and killed.
- June 29, 2005 (Serial Street Shooters)—A horse is shot and killed. David Estrada (20) is shot and killed.
- July 20, 2005 (Serial Street Shooters)—A dog is shot to death.
- Aug 6, 2005 (Baseline Killer)—Goudeau uses a gun to force three teenagers behind a church and proceeds to molest two of them.
- Aug 14, 2005 (Baseline Killer)—Goudeau robs and sexually assaults a woman.
- Sep 8, 2005 (Baseline Killer)—Georgia Thompson (19) is shot and killed by Goudeau.
- Sep 15, 2005 (Baseline Killer)—Goudeau rapes a woman.
- Sep 18, 2005 (Baseline Killer)—Goudeau robs someone at gunpoint.
- Sep 20, 2005 (Baseline Killer)—Goudeau rapes two sisters at gunpoint.
- Sep 28, 2005 (Baseline Killer)—A woman is raped and robbed by Goudeau.
- Nov 3, 2005 (Baseline Killer)—Cupid's Toy Box is robbed and a woman is abducted at gunpoint. Goudeau rapes her before letting her go.
- Nov 7, 2005 (Baseline Killer)—Goudeau robs Las Brasas restaurant, Little Caesar's, and four pedestrians at gunpoint.

- Nov 11, 2005 (Serial Street Shooters)—Nathaniel Schoffner is shot and killed by Hausner. Two dogs are found with gunshot wounds.
- Dec 12, 2005 (Baseline Killer)—Tina Washington (39) is shot and killed behind a restaurant by Goudeau.
- Dec 13, 2005 (Baseline Killer)—A woman is robbed at gunpoint by Goudeau.
- Dec 29, 2005 (Serial Street Shooters)—Barbara Whitener and Timmy Tordai survive being shot. Jose Ortiz (44) and Marco Carillo (28) are shot and killed. Another dog is found shot to death.
- Dec 30, 2005 (Serial Street Shooters)—Clarissa Rowley (21) survives being shot. Three dogs are shot, one of which is killed.
- Feb 20, 2006 (Baseline Killer)—Romelia Vargas (38) and Mirna Palma-Roman (39) are shot to death by Goudeau.
- Mar 15, 2006 (Baseline Killer)—Liliana Sanchez-Cabrera (20) and Chao Chou (23) are carjacked at gunpoint, robbed and then shot to death.
- Mar 29, 2006 (Baseline Killer)—Kristin Nicole Gibbons (26) is killed by Goudeau.
- Apr 10, 2006 (Baseline Killer)—Sophia Nunez is found murdered in her bathtub.
- May 1, 2006 (Baseline Killer)—Goudeau rapes a woman outside of the Las Brasas restaurant he robed in November.
- May 2, 2006 (Serial Street Shooters)—Kibili Tamadul survives being shot by Hausner. Claudia Gutierrez-Cruz (20) is shot and killed by Dieteman.
- May 17, 2006 (Serial Street Shooters)—Timothy Davenport survives being stabbed by Dieteman.
- May 30, 2006 (Serial Street Shooters)—James Hodge is wounded.

- May 31, 2006 (Serial Street Shooters)—Miguel Rodriguez and Davy Davies survive being shot.
- Jun 8, 2006 (Serial Street Shooters)—Arsons at two Wal-Mart stores result in no casualties. Paul Patrick survives being shot.
- Jun 11, 2006 (Serial Street Shooters)—Elizabeth Clark survives being shot.
- Jun 20, 2006 (Serial Street Shooters)—Fredrick Cena and Tony Long survive being shot.
- June 29, 2006 (Baseline Killer)—Carmen Miranda (37) is abducted and then murdered by Goudeau. The crime is caught on a surveillance camera.
- Jul 1, 2006 (Serial Street Shooters)—Diane Bein and Jeremy Ortiz survive being shot.
- Jul 3, 2006 (Serial Street Shooters)—Joseph Roberts survives being shot.
- Jul 7, 2006 (Serial Street Shooters)—David Perez survives being shot.
- Jul 8, 2006 (Serial Street Shooters)—Ashley Armenta and Gary Begay survive being shot.
- Jul 11, 2006 (Serial Street Shooters)—Michael Cordrey survives being shot.
- Jul 11, 2006 (Serial Street Shooters)—Police realize the Serial Street Shooter is actually two people working together, and separately from the Baseline Killer. They are now investigating three active serial killers.
- Jul 22, 2006 (Serial Street Shooters)—Paul Carcia survives being shot.
- Jul 30, 2006 (Serial Street Shooters)—Robert Blasnek (22) is shot and killed by Hausner.
- Aug 3, 2006 (Serial Street Shooters)—Hausner and Dieteman are arrested.
- Aug 6, 2006 (Baseline Killer)—Goudeau molests two girls.
- Sep 4, 2006 (Baseline Killer)—Goudeau is arrested for sexual assault.

The timeline of the 2015-2016 attacks is as follows.

- Aug 12, 2015 (Aaron Saucedo)—A shooting occurs at East Colter Street.
- Aug 16, 2015 (Aaron Saucedo)—Rual Romero (61) dies from multiple gunshot wounds while in his driveway.
- Aug 27, 2015 (Freeway Shootings)—The first vehicle is shot at.
- Sept 10, 2015 (Freeway Shootings)—The last "Freeway Shootings" incident results in at least 11 vehicles struck by gunfire and one injury.
- Sept 13, 2015 (Copycat Shooters)—A group of teenagers are arrested for shooting at cars with pellet guns and slingshots as "copycats" of the Freeway Shootings.
- Sept 28, 2016 (Freeway Shootings)—Leslie Allen Merrit Jr. is arrested as the Freeway Shooter.
- Jan 1, 2016 (Aaron Saucedo)—Jesse Olivas (22) is shot to death while walking down the sidewalk.
- Mar 17, 2016 (Aaron Saucedo)—A 16-year-old boy walking along Moreland Street survives his gunshot wounds.
- Mar 18, 2016 (Aaron Saucedo)—A 21-year-old man is shot while standing next to his vehicle. He survives.
- Apr 1, 2016 (Aaron Saucedo)—Diego Verdugo-Sanchez (21) dies from gunshot wounds while visiting his pregnant fiancé and her family.
- Apr 19, 2016 (Aaron Saucedo)—Krystal Annette White (55) is found deceased from gunshot wounds on 32nd Street.
- Jun 1, 2016 (Aaron Saucedo)—Horacio Pena (32) is shot and killed in his driveway while walking from his vehicle up to his front door.

- Jun 10, 2016 (Aaron Saucedo)—Manuel Castro Garcia (19) is shot and killed outside of his home. A nearby policeman hears the shots, but the killer flees before he arrives on the scene.
- Jun 12, 2016 (Aaron Saucedo)—An unoccupied vehicle on Mariposa Drive is shot at. Around 30 minutes later, Stefanie Ellis (33) and her daughter Maleah (12) are shot and killed while standing outside of their home. Their friend Angela Linner (31) is also shot and eventually succumbs to her wounds, dying three weeks later while in the hospital.
- Jul 11, 2016 (Aaron Saucedo)—A 21-year-old man and 4-year-old boy are in a car that is shot at repeatedly. Both are uninjured.
- Apr 24, 2016- Aaron Saucedo is arrested for the murder of Rual Romero. Ballistics and witness descriptions later connect him to the other shootings.

Further Readings

The Baseline Killer
Book
Crimes of the Centuries: Notorious Crimes, Criminals, and Criminal Trials in American History, Volume 1, Chapter "Mark Goudeau" (starting on page 317) by Steven Chermak Ph.D., Frankie Y. Bailey Ph.D.

Movie
Baseline Killer (2008)

Serial Street Shooters
Book
A Sudden Shot: The Phoenix Serial Shooter by Camille Kimball

Television Show
Monster in my Family, Season 1 Episode 3, "Phoenix Serial Shooter: Dale Hausner"

2005-2006 Phoenix Serial Killings
Books
The Naked Streets: The Shocking True Story of the Phoenix Sniper Murders and Baseline Killer by Ronald Watkins

Serial Shooters: The Rising by Todd A. Hemming

Also by Jack Smith

WRONGFUL
CONVICTIONS
TRUE MURDER CASES
UNBELIEVABLE MISCARRIAGES OF JUSTICE
JACK SMITH

BY PERSON
OR PERSONS...
UNKNOWN
SHEDDING NEW LIGHT ON TRUE UNSOLVED MURDER
MYSTERIES LOST IN TIME BUT NEVER FORGOTTEN
JACK SMITH

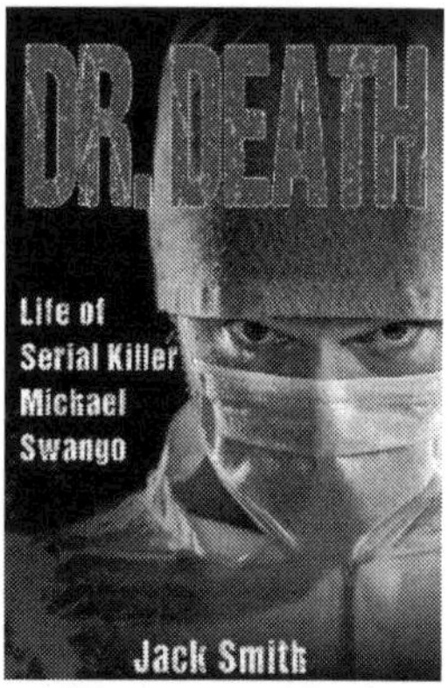
DR. DEATH
Life of
Serial Killer
Michael
Swango
Jack Smith

THE HAPPY FACE
MURDERER
The Life of Serial Killer
Jack Smith

THE HORRIFIC CRIMES
GILLES DE RAIS
REVISITED
Life of a Serial Killer of the Middle Ages
Jack Smith

THE BEAST OF
BIRKENSHAW
LIFE OF SERIAL KILLER
PETER MANUEL
JACK SMITH

BODIES
IN BARRELS
THE SNOWTOWN MURDERS
JACK SMITH

HIDDEN
BRUTALITY
LIFE OF SERIAL KILLER CARL EUGENE WATTS
JACK SMITH

THE SPOKANE
KILLER
Jack Smith

CHRISTMAS
SLAY RIDE
Most Mysterious
and Horrific
Christmas Day Murders
JACK SMITH

THE CROSS COUNTRY
KILLER
Life of Serial Killer Tommy Lynn Sells
Jack Smith

ANGEL OF
DEATH
Life of Serial Killer Tommy Lynn Sells
Jack Smith

Most Mysterious and Headless Unsolved
Murders of All Time
Five Gruesome Unsolved Mysteries
JACK SMITH

The Barton
MURDER
The Mysterious and True
Murder Story on Hamilton
Mountain. Did Someone Get
Away With Murder?
Jack Smith

Printed in Great Britain
by Amazon